GET SMART ABOUT
LIONEL MESSI

Adam Kent

GET SMART ABOUT LIONEL MESSI

ROCKET BOOKS

Get Smart about Lionel Messi
by Adam Kent

Published by Rocket Books, Inc.
New York, NY, USA

Copyright © 2023 Rocket Books, Inc.

All rights reserved. No portion of this book may be reproduced in any form without permission from the publisher, except as permitted by U.S. copyright law. For permissions contact: info@rocketkidsbookclub.com

Disclaimer: Please note the information contained within this document is for educational and entertainment purposes only. All effort has been executed to present accurate, up to date, and reliable, complete information. No warranties of any kind are declared or implied. The content within this book has been derived from different sources. By reading this document the reader agrees that under no circumstances is the author responsible for any losses, direct or indirect, which are incurred as a result of the use of information contained within the document, including, but not limited to, - errors, commissions, or inaccuracies.

ADAM KENT

For kids...
who dream big,
who work hard to become better,
who get up when they fall,
who know we are all human and
all worthy of respect and success.

For my son Little Adam...
who lights up my life.

May your dreams come true.

This book is for you.

GET SMART ABOUT LIONEL MESSI

ABOUT THIS BOOK

This biography book is meant to be a fun, brief and inspirational look at the life of a famous person. Reading biographies can help learn from people who have experienced extraordinary things. While you read through the books in this series, think about how their experiences can help you in your own life!

As you read this book you will find bolded words. There are definitions of the words at the end of each page. You will also find interesting facts at the end of each chapter.

I hope you enjoy learning about this extraordinary person!

Have a great time reading,

Adam Kent

GET SMART ABOUT LIONEL MESSI

CONTENTS

AT A GLANCE 11
FAST FACTS 13
1: THE EARLY DAYS 15
   FUN FACTS 30
2: FAMILY MATTERS 33
   FUN FACTS 43
3: A UNIQUE EDUCATION 45
   FUN FACTS 48
4: A CAREER TO REMEMBER ... 49
   FUN FACTS 77
5: HOBBIES & PASSIONS 79
   FUN FACTS 83
6: A PERSONAL LIFE 85
   FUN FACTS 89
7: A LASTING LEGACY 91
INSPIRATIONAL QUOTES 93
BOOK DISCUSSION 99

GLOSSARY.. **101**
SELECTED REFERENCES................. **109**

ADAM KENT

GET SMART ABOUT
LIONEL
MESSI

Adam Kent

GET SMART ABOUT LIONEL MESSI

LIONEL MESSI
AT A GLANCE

Lionel Messi is one of the greatest footballers of all time. He is most famous for his dazzling skills and record-breaking goals. Yet, it's not just his on-field brilliance that is impressive. Leo's journey from a young boy in Argentina to becoming a global icon is a captivating story. His story reveals the incredible dedication and passion that fuel his success, making you want to uncover the inspiring details of his amazing journey.

GET SMART ABOUT LIONEL MESSI

LIONEL MESSI
FAST FACTS

1. Lionel Messi is considered the GOAT (Greatest of All Time) by many because he broke lots of records and won many awards.

2. He has scored over 700 goals throughout his career so far.

3. People call him "The Flea" because he's so fast and tricky on the field, and some say he's as good as famous players like Pelé and Maradona.

4. Lionel Messi had a growth disorder as a kid, but he didn't give up on his football dreams.

5. He joined FC Barcelona's youth academy, La Masia, at the age of 13, which is very young.

CHAPTER 1
THE EARLY DAYS

Lionel Andrés Messi, one of the greatest footballers of all time, was born on June 24, 1987. He was born in Rosario, Argentina in South America. He was named after one his parents' favorite singers, Lionel Richie, who was also a judge on American Idol. He was given the nickname "Leo." Most of his fans call him "Leo Messi" or just "Messi." We will call him Leo Messi as we get smart about his life!

Leo's early childhood was shaped by a mix of ordinary family life and extraordinary experiences that would eventually **propel** him to stardom.

Leo was the third of four children born to his parents, Jorge Messi and Celia Cuccittini. Jorge, Leo's father, worked as a manager at a steel factory. He worked hard to make sure that the family had a **stable** income. Leo's mother Celia worked in a magnet manufacturing factory. Their **humble** backgrounds provided Leo with the value of hard work, a value that would help him well in his career.

---

propel /prə-'pel/ verb: to make something move faster <example: *The strong wind can propel a kite into the sky.*>'

stable /'stā-bəl/ adjective: when something doesn't change or wobble <example: *The table is stable; it doesn't shake when you touch it.*>

humble /'həm-bəl/ adjective: being modest and not bragging <example: *She's very humble and doesn't show off her toys.*>

Growing up, Leo had two older brothers named Rodrigo and Matías, as well as a sister named Maria. He was close to all of his siblings. The Messis were a close-knit and religious family. They were Christians and part of the Roman Catholic church.

One of the most unique parts about Leo's childhood was his family's great passion for soccer. They loved soccer! All the Messi boys played it constantly growing up. Leo's father was especially fond of the sport. Leo's passion for the sport began at a very young age and was largely influenced by his father.

Let's take a short break to talk about the name "soccer." Soccer is a sport that is also known as "football" and "fútbol." That is why we called Leo a footballer in the beginning of this book. Today, in the United

States, Canada, Australia, and New Zealand, the sport is more often called "soccer," but that seems to be changing over time. Also, in most other countries, it is called "football!" We will call it "football" from now on because that is what Leo called it growing up!

Leo's interest in football was also influenced by his cousins, Maximiliano and Emanuel Biancucchi. Both of them played from a very young age as well. Actually, they also both became professional footballers themselves later on in their life!

When they were all young, Leo, his brothers, and his two cousins all loved playing the sport together. This rich football culture within the family played a big role in creating and driving Leo's love for the game. The practice also helped him develop his skills and talents, preparing him for his later success.

Leo's path to greatness in football more formally began at the age of 4 when he officially joined a local football club in Argentina called Grandoli. Do you know who his first coach was back then? It was his father, Jorge! Yes, his father was his first coach on his first football team as a kid!

Perhaps the most special of **influences** in young Leo's early football path was the support of his grandmother, Celia. Celia shared Leo's love for football and was there for him in every way she could be. In fact, she would take Leo to his early practices and matches all the time and cheer

---

influence /'ın-flu-əns/ noun: when someone or something has the power to change the way you think or act <example: *Her excitement for reading influenced me to start reading more books.*>

him on from the stands. His love for his grandmother is so great that even still when he scores, he points up at the sky in memory of her.

When Leo was just six, he joined a famous football club for youth called Newell's Old Boys. Newell's Old Boys is a sports club in Argentina that was established in 1903. It has teams for many different sports like basketball, hockey, and boxing. The club is famous partly because many professional football players were once members of if it.

Leo played with Newell's for six years. During that time, the budding star **showcased** his big talent by scoring nearly 500 goals! He played in matches for "The Machine of '87." This

---

showcased /SHOH-kayst/ verb: when something is put out for people to see and enjoy *<example: The art gallery showcased beautiful paintings by local artists.>*

was a youth team known for its top performance in Argentina. Leo also entertained audiences during those matches, showing off his ball tricks during half-time!

Leo's journey to football stardom was not without its challenges. At the age of just ten, he received an upsetting **diagnosis** that threatened his dream of becoming a professional footballer. Doctors discovered that he suffered from a growth hormone disorder, also known as GHD. GHD can cause people to stay shorter than average by preventing their growth. It also affects people on the inside. It can affect their eyes, teeth and skin. It can also cause people to be more likely to get sick. For Leo, the disorder raised

---

disorder /dis-OR-der/ noun: when things are not in the right order and can be messy or confused *<example: The messy room was a disorder, with toys everywhere.>*

doubts about his ability to ever compete at the highest level in football.

Leo and his family were **determined** to face the disorder head on. They wanted to give him the best chance at reaching his potential. They didn't want it to set him back, so they investigated all options to treat his disorder. It turned out the best option was for Leo to start taking **injections** of growth hormone to combat the deficiency of it he had. However, the injections were costly, and the family didn't have much money.

---

determined /dee-TUR-mind/ adjective: when you decide to do something and work really hard to make it happen *<example: She was determined to finish the puzzle, so she tried until all the pieces fit together.>*

injections /in-JEK-shuhns/ noun: when the doctor gives you medicine with a special needle to make you feel better *<example: The nurse gave me an injection to help me feel better when I was sick.>*

Leo's father Jorge had health insurance that covered the treatment in the beginning. Unfortunately, it only covered it for two years. Otherwise, the cost would have been at least $1,000 per month. This was too much for the family. At the time, Leo was still playing with Newell's Old Boys. The club was so impressed by Leo's skill and performance in football that they initially agreed to pay for the treatment. However, later they went back on the promise. This was a big **setback** for Leo and the whole Messi family who understood the amazing potential that Leo had in the sport.

The Messi family began looking for other options. They asked other

---

setback /set-bak/ noun when something doesn't go as planned and you face a challenge or obstacle *<example: Missing the school bus was a setback, but I decided to walk to school instead.>*

local clubs in Argentina if they would like Leo to play for them and would be willing to cover the expenses of the treatment but struck out. They then started looking outside of Argentina.

In 2000, an agent from Argentina named Horacio Gaggioli who believed in Leo's special talent reached out to a club in Barcelona, Spain, in Europe, called FC Barcelona. The club's first-team director, Charly Rexach, **hesitated** at first. Leo was young. Usually, the club signed teens around the age of 17 or 18. Charly knew that it would be difficult to get approval for signing Leo because of his age. But Horacio talked up Leo so much that he finally agreed to arrange for Messi and his family to travel to Barcelona so

---

hesitated /hez-i-tey-tid/ verb: when you stop or pause before doing something *<example: He hesitated before jumping into the cold water.>*

that Leo could try out for a couple of weeks.

When Charly finally saw Leo play, he thought he was absolutely amazing! He was so impressed by Leo's talent that he feared if he didn't sign him, he may have ended up being the guy who didn't sign a future star! He saw that on the field, Leo seemed to always have the ball. He was brave. He was courageous. He was a star.

Charly decided to sign Leo. You might be surprised by how the director offered Leo his first contract, though. Leo's father had pressured Charly during a meeting to decide about Leo. On the spot, Charly presented an offer using a napkin since that is all that was around him. Yes, Leo's offer was first written on a paper napkin!

In February 2001, the Messi family made a life-changing decision. They believed in Leo and wanted to support him fully. So, the family decided to temporarily relocate to Barcelona, Spain in order to pursue Leo's dreams! That is **dedication**!

The family moved into an apartment near Camp Nou, which is Barcelona's most famous football stadium. This move marked the beginning of Leo's journey to superstardom. The location of the apartment served as a reminder of the reason for the move and **motivated** Leo to push harder and harder to reach his dreams.

Leo's first year in Spain was

---

dedication /ded-i-key-shuhn/ noun: when you work really hard and put a lot of effort into something <example: *Her dedication to practicing the piano every day made her a great musician.*>

motivated /moh-tuh-vey-tid/ adjective: when you feel excited and eager to do something <example: *He was motivated to finish his homework so he could go play outside.*>

hard. He missed Argentina. He also had to **adapt** to a new country and learn a new language. In Barcelona, Spanish is spoken, just like in Argentina, but people also speak a language called Catalan which is a variation of Spanish. Leo had to learn Catalan. Also, his mother and siblings moved back to Rosario in Argentina. His father stayed in Barcelona to support Leo, but the separation from the rest of the family proved hard for young Leo.

In Barcelona, Leo joined the youth academy at FC Barcelona called La Masia. Adjusting to the academy was hard for Leo. Leo was a pretty quiet boy at the time. The new country and language challenged him. Some of his

---

adapt /uh-dapt/ verb: when you change and find new ways to do something to fit the situation <example: Birds adapt to different weather by growing thicker feathers in the winter.>

teammates in Barcelona even wondered at first if Leo was **mute**, since he barely talked! It also took about a year for Leo to be able to start playing in competitions, which was what he loved most.

In February of 2002, after about a year at the academy, Leo was officially enrolled in the Royal Spanish Football Federation (RFEF) and allowed to start playing in competitions. Leo quickly became a top player in Barcelona's youth **division**. During his first full season he became the top scorer! He also made friends with his teammates,

---

division /dih-vizh-uhn/ noun: when something is separated or split into parts *<example: The division of the cake into equal slices made it easy to share with everyone.>*

mute /myoot/ adjective: when something doesn't make a sound or is very quiet *<example: The mute button on the TV remote makes the sound go away.>*

among whom were Cesc Fàbregas and Gerard Piqué who also became professional players. Because the team was so good, they were called the "Baby Dream Team."

Overall, Leo Messi's early childhood was marked by a loving family, a passion for football, and the challenge of a growth hormone deficiency. His parents' support, his grandmother's influence, and his strong determination paved the way for his remarkable journey from a young boy with a dream to one of the greatest footballers the world has ever seen.

CHAPTER 1
FUN FACTS

1. Leo Messi's love for football started when he was just a toddler. He began playing football at the tender age of three and quickly displayed his extraordinary skills even then.

2. Lionel Messi's nickname, "Leo," is a shortened version of his full name. It's a common practice in Argentina to use a shortened form of a person's name.

3. When Leo scores today, he points up to the sky in memory of his beloved grandmother.

4. At the age of 10, Messi was diagnosed with a growth hormone deficiency that would have likely caused him to grow to about four and a half feet only.

5. The required treatment cost for hormone injections to treat his disorder was about $1,000 per month.

6. Leo joined the football club in Spain called FC Barcelona at a very young age - just 13!

GET SMART ABOUT LIONEL MESSI

CHAPTER 2
FAMILY MATTERS

Leo Messi grew up in Argentina in a close-knit family made up of his mother and father and three siblings. Leo's father was named Jorge Messi. He was born on April 1, 1958, in Rosario, Argentina. His mother was Celia Cuccittini. She was born on January 18, 1960, in Rosario, as well.

Leo's father Jorge is a really important person in his life and always has been. Before Leo became famous, Jorge worked as a supervisor at the Acindar metal works factory in Rosario. The Messi family was not wealthy or poor. Besides being a hard factory worker, Jorge had another important and special job. He was Leo's very first football coach at the local sports club called the Grandoli club! He taught his son how to play the game and helped him become really good at it!

Over the years, as Leo's skills grew and he started catching the eye of coaches, Jorge's role changed. He became not just a coach but also a mentor and **advisor** to his son. Actually, since the early 2000s, Jorge has officially been Leo's agent and manager. That means he helps with

---

advisor /uhd-vahy-zer/ noun: someone who gives advice or helps you with information or guidance <example: My teacher is a helpful advisor; she gives me advice on my school projects.>

important decisions about contracts, business deals, and Leo's career.

Even though Jorge's support for his son has always been strong, it hasn't always been easy for other people involved in Leo's career. Some people say that Jorge got too involved in Leo's football career. That sometimes caused problems when dealing with football clubs and other advisors. But no matter what, Jorge always wanted what was best for his Leo and fought hard for him.

Jorge Messi hasn't just been involved in Leo's football career; he's also been a big part of his business deals with big companies like Adidas, Pepsi, and Mastercard that came out of Leo's amazing career. These deals have made the Messi family very wealthy.

Some people have different opinions about how Jorge manages

things, but there's no doubt that he's always been dedicated to making sure his son succeeds. He has been like a guide, mentor, and manager on Leo's incredible journey from a small town in Argentina to becoming one of the world's greatest football players ever.

Leo's mom, Celia, has also been an important person in his life as well. Celia was always a loving and dedicated mother to her children. She worked at a magnet manufacturing workshop when Leo was a kid to help provide for the family. She showed her commitment to their well-being by working hard to earn an extra income for the family. Her hard work and sacrifices were necessary to making sure that Leo had the support he needed to pursue his dreams.

As Leo's football journey took off, Celia's role became more than just a caring provider. She became his supporter too, attending his matches and cheering him on from the sidelines. Her constant presence served as motivation for Leo, driving him to succeed.

Celia also made hard decisions that were best for Leo and the family. When Leo faced the challenge of having to find a club that could pay for his hormone injections, Celia supported his move to Barcelona. She stayed back in Rosalio to take care of the rest of the family, while Jorge and Leo were in Barcelona. Being away from her husband and son was hard. However, it was necessary for Leo to be able to get his treatments and pursue his dreams, while still making sure the rest of the family had enough money and a sense of home.

Throughout Leo's rise to stardom, Celia remained humble. Even when Leo had become famous, she stayed out of the spotlight. She allowed Leo to shine bright. She provided motherly support behind the scenes, while taking care of the rest of the family too. Celia continued to show the values of **humility**, hard work, and family. She serves as a shining example of the big impact a mother's love and support can have on a child's life. Her firm belief in Leo's **potential**, as well as her sacrifices, have played a significant role in shaping him into the football legend the world admires today.

Leo also has two older brothers, named Matias and Rodrigo. Matias was

---

humility /hyoo-mil-i-tee/ noun: when someone is modest and doesn't show off or act better than others *<example: His humility made him well-liked by everyone.*

potential /puh-ten-shuhl/ noun: when you have the ability to do something well in the future *<example: With hard work and practice, you can reach your full potential and achieve your goals.>*

born on October 1, 1982. Rodrigo was born on February 10, 1988. Leo has a younger sister named Maria Sol, as well. She was born on November 30, 1993.

Leo shares a deep and heartwarming bond with his brothers. That bond has been a source of strength throughout his life. Rodrigo and Matias also played big roles in shaping his character and nurturing his love for football.

From a young age, the Messi brothers would spend countless hours playing football together in the streets of their neighborhood in Argentina. These early experiences not only helped Leo develop his skills, but they also helped Leo develop a healthy competitive spirit and determination that helped his future career. Playing with his older brother's also helped him develop the confidence to play against much older people, which helped him during his trial in Barcelona. Rodrigo and Matias also acted as both mentors and supporters. They recognized Leo's exceptional talent and encouraged him to pursue his dreams.

As Leo's career skyrocketed, his bond with his brothers remained unbreakable. They continue to attend his matches and celebrate his achievements. They also became involved in advising his game and managing his businesses throughout the years. The close relationship between the brothers helped shape Leo Messi into the football **icon** we know today.

Leo's relationship with his sister

---

icon /ahy-kon/ noun: a symbol or person who is widely recognized and represents something special or important <example: *Mickey Mouse is an icon of Disney, known and loved by people all over the world.*>

Maria was loving. As the youngest and only girl in the family she was the princess! Her brothers shared a deep love of football and were older. Also, Leo moved to Barcelona when she was young. However, Maria has still had a close bond with Leo and his brothers.

Maria has also helped Leo with his businesses as an adult too. She is the brand manager of the Messi Store. The Messi Store is a Leo's online clothing store. She even worked directly with the store's previous creative director, Ginny Hilfiger. The creative director is the boss of cool ideas and making sure things in the business look great. Ginny Hilfiger is the younger sister of the world-famous fashion designer Tommy Hilfiger!

Leo Messi's family played a huge role in helping him become the amazing footballer he is. They spent a lot of time playing football with him when he was a kid, which helped him get really good at it. Later, they supported him and worked with him to build his career and businesses. More than that, they taught him important things like never giving up and working together as a team. Messi's family always believed in him, and that belief helped him achieve incredible success in his career.

CHAPTER 2
FUN FACTS

1. Leo Messi played football with his two older brothers from a very young age. This is one of the reasons he was so amazing at football from a young age.

2. Leo's father Jorge was his first football coach in the local club in Argentina called the Grandioli club.

3. Leo's father later became his agent and has been throughout his career.

4. Leo's sister Maria manages the family's online clothing store called "The Messi Store" and once

worked with the sister of Tommy Hilfiger, Ginny, who was the creative director for the store.

5. Leo's cousins, Maximiliano and Emanuel Biancucchi, are also professional footballers.

CHAPTER 3
A UNIQUE EDUCATION

Leo Messi's education was unique. While his early years were marked by a love for football, his family knew that a solid education was equally important.

Leo's formal schooling began at "Escuela No 66 Las Heras," a public elementary school in his hometown of Rosario, Argentina. As a young student, he showed not only a love for football but also a commitment to his studies. His teachers noted his hard work and intelligence, qualities that extended beyond the football field.

However, when Leo was just 13 years old, a big change came. He and his family decided to move to Spain so that he could join the youth academy of FC Barcelona, known as La Masia. This was a big turning point in his life. It was the beginning of his professional football career! But it also was a big **disruption** in his education.

In Spain, Messi continued his education at Instituto Joan Miró, a high school in Barcelona. This was no easy task! He had to balance intense football training with his school responsibilities. His teachers

---

disruption /dis-ruhp-shuhn/ noun: when something interrupts or changes the normal way of doing things <example: *The loud noise outside caused a disruption in our class, making it hard to concentrate on our lessons.*>

saw his exceptional situation and cahnged his schedule so that he could meet his training responsibilities for FC Barcelona. Even with these challenges, Leo knew he wanted to complete his high school education and earn his diploma! This showed his belief in the value of education.

What sets Leo's education journey apart is his ability to do great both on and off the field. He showed that it's possible to chase your dreams while also valuing education. Leo knew that education is an important part of success.

CHAPTER 3
FUN FACTS

1. Leo moved to Spain at the age of 13 to join FC Barcelona's youth academy, La Masia.

2. Leo had to learn a language called Catalan in Spain.

3. Leo's teachers in Spain adjusted his schedule to accommodate his football schedule.

4. Leo successfully earned his high school diploma, highlighting his commitment to education.

CHAPTER 4
A CAREER TO REMEMBER

Leo Messi's career took off when he joined Barcelona's youth academy, La Masia, at a young age. His journey in Barcelona was nothing short of spectacular. At La Masia, he quickly formed friendships with fellow talented players who later became professional players as well. He also trained hard.

In February 2002, after a year of training, Messi officially became a part of the Royal Spanish Football

Federation (RFEF). Thus, he was able to play in games! Soon he became part of what was called the "Baby Dream Team." This nickname was given to a group of talented young players who came up through the ranks of Barcelona's youth academy around the same time as Leo. The "Baby Dream Team" included not just Leo, but other players like Gerard Piqué, Cesc Fàbregas, and others. These players achieved great success at the youth level. They won numerous competitions. They were seen as the future of Barcelona's "first team," which is the professional team.

During the 2003-04 season, Leo's fourth year at La Masia, he rose through the ranks of the youth teams quickly. He first was a starter with a team called "Juvenil B." A starter is a player who plays right when a game begins. Starters are usually considered to be the top players and also play most of the game as well. Soon after, he was named the "player of the competition" in several games. Since he did so well, he was moved up to the Juvenil A team, which is the highest youth team. Higher than that team is the first team.

Leo's talent was noticed. He was quickly added to the first team to train during the season break when other first team players were weakened. This marked his first team debut at just 16 years old! Typically, Juvenil B players range from 16-18 years old and Juvenil A players range from 18-19, so Leo was very young to have moved up beyond those levels to the first team!

Club vs. National Teams

Before we continue with Leo's career, there is something important to know. In football there are many different competitions or tournaments. These competitions fall in two large groups: club or national. A player has to be part of a sports club, like FC Barcelona (or just "Barcelona"), to play in club games. Club competitions can be against other clubs in one country or around the world.

On the other hand, to play in national competitions, usually a player has to be a citizen of the country they play for. If they are a citizen for two countries, then often the player can choose which country's team to join.

Around 2003, when managers in Spain started to notice what a star Leo was, they tried to get him to play for Spain on the national team and not just Barcelona, the club team. He would become a Spanish citizen one day. However, Argentina wanted to keep Leo as well! In the end, Leo decided to play for Argentina, since it was his home country. So, Leo played for Argentina in national competitions like the FIFA World Cup and Copa America. They usually happen every four years. OK! Let's get back to Barcelona!

First Team

At the young age of 16, Leo Messi was training with the first team in Barcelona. It is also known as the senior team. It is the top-level professional team at FC Barcelona that includes the club's best players who compete in professional competitions. They represent FC Barcelona in La Liga (the top Spanish competition) and others. Players in the first team have reached the highest level in their careers. ...And Leo was amongst these players at just 16! Can you believe it?

To help explain just how **impressive** Leo was at a young age, during one training session with the first team, a French player named Ludovic Guily described Leo's playing by saying, "He destroyed us all... They were kicking him all over the place to avoid being ridiculed by this kid, he just got up and kept on playing. He would dribble past four players and score a goal. Even the team's starting center-backs were nervous. He was an alien." That is an amazing compliment! He performed so well that he was also added to Barcelona's reserve team called Barcelona B.

One of the most notable aspects of Leo's early career at Barcelona was the support and friendship he received

---

impressive /im-pres-iv/ adjective: when something makes a strong and positive impact, often because it's really good or big *<example: The amazing fireworks show was truly impressive.>*

from Ronaldinho, the team's star player at the time. That first year, Ronaldinho called Leo his "little brother," and even told other players that he thought one day Leo would become even better than him!

First Contract

Leo Messi's rapid rise led to his first professional contract. It wasn't for the first team, but it was a big deal. It meant he was also going to be paid a lot of money to play! The contract was signed in February 2004 and lasted until 2012. To give you an idea of how much money we are talking about, it included a buyout of €30 million. "€" stands for Euros, which is a currency of Europe. This meant that if another team wanted Leo to play with them, they would have to pay FC Barcelona over $30 mil to get him.

A month after signing his first contract, Leo made his debut for Barcelona B. He was smaller than many of his opponents, so he focused on increasing his strength. That helped him **excel** on the field. In the 2004-05 season, Messi was a regular starter for Barcelona B, playing in 17 games and scoring 6 goals. His performances were noticed by the senior players. They asked their manager, Frank Rijkaard, to put Leo in first team games. He did!

On May 1, 2005, Messi scored his first senior goal for Barcelona in a match against Albacete, which is also in Spain. He became the youngest-ever scorer for the club! Barcelona won the league that season, marking their first league title in six years.

---

excel /ik-sel/ verb: when you are very good at something or do it better than others *<example: She worked hard to excel in her studies and got top grades in her class.>*

First Senior Team Contract

On June 24th, 2005, a huge day for any young footballer, Leo Messi signed his first senior team contract with FC Barcelona. It happened on the day he turned 18. It didn't last as long though. It was for just two years. However, the new buy out price was €150 million!

By then, people started realizing what a star Leo was. One big moment for Leo came on August 24th, 2005. He was a starter in a match for the first time. He took center stage in front of the world. His playing earned him a standing ovation from at the stadium in Barcelona, which is called Camp Nou.

Fabio Capello, the manager of the competing team, was so impressed by Leo's skills during that game that he asked about bringing Leo to his team in Italy! Can you believe it? Capello even said of young Leo then, "In my entire life I have never seen a player of such quality and personality at such a young age, particularly wearing the 'heavy' shirt of one of the world's great clubs."

At the same time, Inter Milan, a club from Italy, made a buyout offer of €150 million! That was his actual buyout price! They also offered to triple his salary. Leo turned the offers down. He decided to stay and continue his journey with Barcelona. They thanked him by extending his contract to 2014.

Leo quickly became the first-choice right winger for the team. He was wearing a number 19 shirt at the time. During games he worked as a team with players Ronaldinho and Samuel Eto'o on the field. In Spain, there is a yearly competition in Spain called La Liga (the League). 20 teams compete for the first-place title. FC Barcelona won during the 2005-06 season with the help of Leo!

Leo continued to shine in the following years. During the 2006-07 season, he became one of the world's best players. He scored 17 goals in 36 games. He also struggled with injuries as well. Sometimes they were big enough that he had to stop playing for months, which really frustrated him. This comes with playing the game though.

Despite the injuries, his impact on the team was **undeniable**. Barcelona wasn't doing as well as a team though. This was partly due to Leo's injuries and not being able to play. However, his rise to football stardom was clear.

---

undeniable /uhn-di-nahy-uh-buhl/ adjective: when something is impossible to deny or argue against *<example: The evidence presented in the case was undeniable; it clearly proved his guilt.>*

Number 10

After two not-so-great seasons, Barcelona decided to make some big changes. They said goodbye to their coach, Frank Rijkaard, and their star player, Ronaldinho. In 2008, Messi was given the number 10 shirt, a significant honor in football. It is often given to the player who will lead the team on the field. Many amazing players have had that number in history including Pele and Ronaldinho!

Leo was also given a new contract. This one made him the highest-paid player at the club. He was given a yearly salary of €7.8 million.

Ballon d'Or

In the 2008-09 season, Messi had a fantastic run. He scored 38 goals in 51 games! This was a club record at the time! Under the new coach, Leo was given more freedom to move around on the field and create chances to score. It worked!

That season, Leo helped Barcelona win their first-ever treble, which means they won three big trophies in one season: La Liga (a Spanish competition), La Copa del Rey (another Spanish competition), and Champions League (a competition in Europe for club teams). After, Leo was given another contract until 2016. His pay increased even more! In the second half of 2009, Barcelona kept winning, and they became the first club ever to win six major trophies in one year! This included the FIFA Club World Cup, where Leo scored the winning goal!

In case you don't know, the FIFA Club World Cup is a worldwide competition of club teams. It is different from the FIFA World Cup, which is a worldwide competition of national teams. The FIFA World Cup is the most **prestigious** competition in international football. It's often considered the pinnacle of football, with billions of viewers and enormous global attention. Now back to his journey!

To add to his amazing success at only 22 years old, Leo was also awarded the Ballon d'Or and FIFA World Player of the Year! Ballon d'Or ("Golden Ball" in English) is an award from France that has been given every year to the best player in the world since 1956. It is one of the biggest honors a player can get!

---

prestigious /pri-stij-uhs/ adjective: when something is respected and admired because it's considered important or of high quality <*example: Graduating from a prestigious university can open up many opportunities in your career.*>

Leo played great during the 2009-10 season and scored 47 goals. He was Barcelona's top scorer in the Champions League. Barcelona won La Liga again. Also, Messi received his first European Golden Shoe award for being the top goal scorer in Europe! This period was when he truly became one of the greatest footballers ever.

During the 2010-11 season, Leo played well again. He helped Barcelona win the Supercopa de España (Super Cup of Spain) with a "hat-trick." A hat trick is when a player scores three goals in one game. From 2010 to 2015, FIFA and French Football combined their awards into one: FIFA Ballon d'Or. After that, they gave them separately again. In 2010, Leo also won the first-ever FIFA Ballon d'Or award! This season, Messi also scored an impressive 53 goals in all, marking his place as a football legend.

Breaking Records

The following years we all about breaking more records for Leo. During the 2011-12 season, he scored 73 goals and helped win the Spanish and European Super Cups. He also achieved something amazing by scoring 5 goals in a single Champions League game, a feat never seen before in the competition's history. On March 20, 2012, Leo also became Barcelona's all-time top scorer at just 24 years old, breaking a 57-year-old record! And won his third Ballon d'Or!

During the 2012-2013 season, Leo officially set two records for the Guinness Book of World Records. He set the record for the "Most Goals in a Calendar Year" by scoring 91 goals for both Barcelona and the Argentina national team in 2012. He also won the "Most Consecutive FIFA Ballon d'Or

Wins" by winning the award for the fourth time in 2021. "Consecutive" means all in a row. He had won it every year from 2009 to 2012, marking the longest winning streak in the history of the award. He also extended his contract until 2018 and became the team's captain in March. What a year!

In 2013-14, Leo faced doubts about his playing due to injuries, but still became Barcelona's top scorer again! Despite this, Barcelona ended the season without major trophies. Still, Leo signed a new contract in May 2014 amid interest from other clubs and got another big pay increase.

In the 2014-15 season, Leo helped Barcelona win the treble again, taking the title in La Liga, the Copa del Rey, and the UEFA Champions League, which is a big European competition also known as "'the Euro." Leo didn't play for that competition because it is a national competition. However, he helped win the others and scored 43 goals total.

During 2015-16 season Leo became injured again. He couldn't play for several weeks. However, in true Leo form, he still managed to score 41 goals and help Barcelona win the La Liga title and the Copa del Rey. They fell short in the Champions League, finishing as runners-up, which means second place.

In the 2016-17 season, Leo Messi continued his exceptional journey with Barcelona. The peak of the season was that he scored his 500th goal for Barcelona! He finished the year as Europe's top scorer.

In the 2017-18 season, he helped Barcelona secure the La Liga and Copa del Rey titles. A significant milestone came when he celebrated his 400th La Liga game. The 2018-19 season marked his 400th La Liga goal and his 600th Barcelona goal! The next season, 2019-20, he faced injury setbacks again, but still played well. By then, Leo had also won his sixth Ballon d'Or! After a great run for many years, a big change was about to happen...

The Big Change

By 2020, Leo Messi had decided he wanted to leave FC Barcelona. He wasn't happy with changes he saw on and off the field. On August 25, 2020, he asked to leave. This caused the press to go wild. But leaving wasn't made easy for Leo. Barcelona's sporting director, Ramon Planes, stated that FC Barcelona still planned to "build a team around the most important player in the world" and insisted there was a €700 million buyout clause! There was a disagreement over whether a part of Leo's contract allowed him to leave for free. However, Leo decided to stay for the final year of his contract in order to avoid a fight. He said at the time, "I would never go to court against the club of my life." This showed his loyalty to Barcelona. Leo played for one final season with Barcelona.

Here are some of Leo's stats from his time with Barcelona:

- 672 goals
- 35 major trophies
    - 4 UEFA Champions League titles
    - 10 La Liga titles
    - 7 Copa del Rey titles
- 778 games

Paris Saint-Germain (PSG) and Inter Miami

After leaving Barcelona, Leo Messi joined the French club team called Paris Saint-Germain (PSG) in August 2021. He struggled in his debut season. He faced challenges on and off the field. However, he still won his seventh Ballon d'Or award.

In his second season with PSG, from 2022-2023, Leo still struggled with the team. Also, he was suspended after taking a trip to Saudi Arabia when he was supposed to be training. The club announced it would be his last season with PSG. Still, by the end of it, he had become the all-time highest goal scorer in European club football.

After leaving PSG, there were rumors that Leo might join the club team in Saudi Arabia or go back to Barcelona. However, he ended up signing a contract with Inter Miami in Florida, USA. He signed a contract there for two and a half years. His first game was on August 26, 2023. He scored and helped the club end an 11-game losing streak! It remains to be seen how many more records Leo will break in club games, but it will be exciting to watch!

FIFA World Cup

So far, we have learned a lot about Leo Messi's club career. However, you may recall that he also played for Argentina over the years in national competitions, like the FIFA World Cup and the Copa America, which is a competition in South America. These are competitions that now run every four years. Let's learn a little about how Leo did in these competitions.

Unfortunately, in 2016, Argentina had been on a streak of not winning either the FIFA World Cup or the Copa America since 1993. In 2005, Leo made his senior debut for the national team. From then on, he had the attention of Argentinian football fans. They hoped this star would help Argentina win again.

Throughout the 2000s, Leo was a key player in Argentina's national team. He **showcased** his incredible dribbling skills, vision, and goal-scoring ability. He was part of the team that won the 2005 FIFA World Youth Championship and the 2008 Beijing Olympics.

However, it was in the senior national team that Leo faced the

---

showcased /shoh-kayst/ verb: when something is displayed or presented for others to see and appreciate <example: *The art gallery showcased beautiful paintings by local artists.*>

biggest pressure. 2016 was an especially hard year for Leo. He got penalties and didn't play as well as he wanted. To make matters worse, Argentina lost both big titles again. There was a lot of pressure on Leo to save Argentina and help them win. He was disappointed in himself and frustrated. Also, the public in Argentina had even started to question him. It all took an emotional toll on him. This caused him to make a surprising announcement. He announced his retirement from international football and playing for Argentina!

The public in Argentina didn't like that idea at all! In fact, they **campaigned** to get him to change his

---

campaigned /kam-peynd/ verb: when someone actively works to promote a cause or run for a position, like in an election <example: *He campaigned to win the student council election, talking to classmates and sharing his ideas.*>

mind, big time! The president of Argentina, Mauricio Macri, publicly asked him to stay. The mayor of Buenos Aires, the capital of Argentina, even put up a statue of him in the city. Also, 50,000 fans went on the streets together with signs encouraging him to stay. It was unbelievable! And guess what... It worked! He decided to stay!

After returning to play in the national team with Argentina, the team continued to struggle to win. The dry streak since 1993 continued. However, in July of 2021, with the big help of Leo, Argentina finally broke its streak and won the Copa America! The fans were happy! All they wanted now was the biggest win of all: the FIFA World Cup.

FIFA World Cup

The 2022 FIFA World Cup took place in Qatar. Qatar is a small country in the Middle East. The final game took place on December 18, 2022. It was an **intense** game. Argentina played against France. Leo scored two points. Then, an amazing player named Kylian Mbappé (say Em-bah-pay) scored two goals also. Then, Leo scored again. And then, in the last two minutes of the game, Mbappé scored again, tying the game!

The game went into overtime, which means they had to play longer than normal. Then, it went into extra-time! Neither team scored. So, it went to a penalty shoot-out between Leo and Mbappé. That means two players try to finish the game by taking turns kicking to score goals with no one else on the field but the goalie. Leo scored

---

intense /in-tens/ adjective: when something is very strong or extreme, often causing strong feelings or reactions *<example: The thunderstorm was so intense that it made everyone stay inside until it passed.>*

4 goals and Mbappé scored 2 in the shootout. Do you know what that means? It means that Argentina won the 2022 FIFA World Cup! The game was seen as one of the best of all time. What a victory!

The Messi Brand

Throughout his football career, with the help of his father who was his manager and his brothers, Leo used his star power to make a lot of money and also do good, which we will learn about later. Many sports brands wanted Leo to represent them advertisements. Over the years, Leo has worked with brands like Adidas, Nike, Pepsi, Dolce & Gabbana (a fashion brand), and Hard Rock Cafe. His face was the cover of video games. He also has an online store called the Messi Store, which his sister Maria runs.

He made a lot of money! In 2019, Forbes magazine named him the highest paid athlete in the world. And by 2020 he was the second athlete ever in a team sport, behind Cristiano Ronaldo to make over $1,000,000,000,000. That is a BILLION dollars. All this from a little boy from Argentina with a big dream and a lot of determination!

CHAPTER 4
FUN FACTS

1. Leo Messi played soccer for a team called FC Barcelona for a long time. He scored more goals for them than anyone else in the team's history. He's like a scoring superstar!

2. When Leo was only 17, he became the youngest player to score a goal for the FC Barcelona team.

3. Leo is the captain of the Argentina national soccer team. He helped his team win the Copa America in 2021 and the FIFA World Cup in 2022.

4. He holds the record for scoring the most goals in a single season in Europe's top leagues.

5. Leo is not just a soccer star; he also helps kids in need. He started a foundation that supports children's education and healthcare. He's a real-life superhero off the field!

CHAPTER 5
HOBBIES AND PASSIONS

Beyond his outstanding football career, Leo Messi has a variety of hobbies and passions. One of Messi's big passions is **charity** work. He established the Leo Messi Foundation in 2007, aiming to provide education, healthcare, and sports opportunities to

---

charity /cher-i-tee/ noun: when people or organizations help others in need, often by giving money, goods, or their time <*example: Donating to a charity helps provide food and clothing to those less fortunate in our community.*>

children in need. Messi has donated millions to this foundation and actively participates in its projects. He's been involved in projects such as building classrooms in Nepal, providing medical supplies to children in need, and supporting youth sports programs. It is truly amazing how much he has helped children.

Messi is also an avid collector. He likes to collect football memorabilia. He has an extensive collection of jerseys, boots, and other football-related items, including souvenirs from some of the sport's biggest moments. This passion for collecting shows his deep love for the game and its history.

Believe it or not, Messi also enjoys video games. Can you guess what type he likes? If you guessed sports, you are right! He especially likes playing FIFA and Pro Evolution Football. He expressed his interest in these games publicly, even appearing on the cover of the Pro Evolution Football series. Playing video games provides him with a fun and relaxing way to unwind and connect with friends. It also helps him come up with ideas to use on the field!

Another lesser-known passion of Messi is his love for **cuisine**. He's a food lover who enjoys cooking and tasting different foods. In fact, he even opened a restaurant called Bellavista del Jardín del Norte in Barcelona. They offer both Argentinian and Mediterranean style food.

As you can see, most of Leo's hobbies and passions are actually related to his biggest passion of all outside of this family: football!

---

cuisine /kwi-zeen/ noun: a style of cooking or food preparation, often associated with a specific region or culture <example: *Italian cuisine is famous for its delicious pasta dishes and pizza.*>

However, they also show that Messi cares about the world and wants to make it a better richer place, either through his honorable charitable causes or by introducing people to delicious foods from about the world.

CHAPTER 5
FUN FACTS

1. Leo Messi is known for his humility as well as his incredible football talent.

2. Leo collects football jerseys from legends like Pelé and Maradona.

3. He's a fan of playing video games.

4. He has tattoos, including his wife's eye, his son's handprint, and the number 10. All of his tattoos have special meaning to him.

GET SMART ABOUT LIONEL MESSI

CHAPTER 6
A PERSONAL LIFE

Leo Messi is married and has three beautiful children. His wife is named Antonela Roccuzzo. Actually, she has been a big part of his life since they were children! Antolela's cousin is Leo's best friend from childhood. His name is Lucas Scaglia He also happens to be a professional football player.

Leo first met Antoella at a football game when Antoella's cousin introduced her to Leo after a football game when Leo was just 5! Leo moved to Barcelona at 13 years old, so they didn't see each other much after that, but kept in touch. However, in 2005 a friend of Antonella's died in a car crash. She was so upset that Leo flew all the way to Argentina to support her!

The couple started to date shortly after, but they kept it secret. They wanted to get to know each other without worrying about what the public thought. Leo first talked about their relationship publicly in an interview in 2009.

In 2010, their love story took a significant turn when Leo proposed to Antonella. They got married on June 30, 2017, in a grand ceremony in Rosario. This event was considered the "wedding of the century" in Argentina. Football players and celebrities like pop-singer Shakira attended.

Leo Messi and Antonela Roccuzzo have been blessed with three wonderful sons who have brought joy to their lives. Their firstborn, Thiago, was born in 2012. Their second son, Mateo, was born in 2015. Finally, their third son, Ciro was born in 2018.

Thiago, Leo's oldest son, has followed in his father's footsteps. He even joined the same sports academy his father played in! Later, he joined an academy in France, and in 2023, he joined Inter Miami, an academy in Florida, USA. Will he grow up to become a professional player like his father? We will have to find out!

Leo is close with his wife and sons. Even though he is so busy, he tries to balance his life with quality family time. Leo said during an interview with a media company called Marca in 2019 that even though they don't have much quiet time at home with three kids, they try to enjoy every second with them. They watch TV, play and just stay at home to make sure they get the most out of their time together as a family.

CHAPTER 6
FUN FACTS

1. Leo Messi met his wife, Antonela Roccoozzo, during his childhood in Rosario, Argentina.

2. Leo and Antonela have three sons: Thiago, Mateo, and Ciro.

3. Thiago Messi, Leo's oldest son, plays for youth football academies just like his father did.

4. Leo and Antonela's wedding in Rosario, Argentina. It was a star-studded event. Shakira the pop singer even attended.

GET SMART ABOUT LIONEL MESSI

CHAPTER 7
A LASTING LEGACY

Leo Messi's legacy is truly amazing. On the football field, his career is nothing short of legendary. He has set numerous records, won multiple Ballon d'Or awards, and changed what it means to be a football superstar. Off the field, Leo's legacy is equally impressive. His charitable work through the Leo Messi Foundation has touched countless lives, supporting education and healthcare for those in need. Family also plays a significant part in his legacy. Leo's powerful love for his wife Antonela and their three children shows his commitment to family. Even as he continues his amazing journey, Leo's passion for the game continues to captivate fans. His legacy goes beyond football. It is about excellence, humility, charity, and family values. Leo Messi has truly left an unforgettable mark on the world.

ADAM KENT

INSPIRATIONAL QUOTES

Quotes are like magical words that can lift your spirits and make you feel like you can conquer the world! They are short and powerful sentences that carry big messages. Quotes come from inspiring people who have experienced many things in life. They teach us valuable lessons, remind us to be brave, and encourage us to follow our dreams.

So, whenever you need some inspiration or a little boost of confidence, just read a quote, and you'll feel like you can achieve anything! Here are a few quotes from Leo Messi to inspire you on your way!

❝ I start early, and I stay late, day after day, year after year. It took me 17 years and 114 days to become an overnight success."

❝ Football is my passion and not my job."

❝ The best decisions aren't made with your mind, but with your instincts."

> Money is not a motivating factor. Money doesn't thrill me or make me play better because there are benefits to being wealthy. I'm just happy with a ball at my feet. My motivation comes from playing the game I love."

> There's nothing more satisfying than seeing a happy and smiling child. I always help in any way I can, even if it's just by signing an autograph."

> The day you think there are no improvements to be made is a sad one for any player."

> I have fun like a child in the street. When the day comes when I'm not enjoying it, I will leave football."

> You can overcome anything, if and only if you love something enough."

> I don't need the best hairstyle or the best body. Just give me a ball at my feet, and I'll show you what I can do."

> In football, the worst things are excuses."

> I am competitive and I feel bad when we lose. You can see it in me when we've lost. I'm in a bad way. I don't like to talk to anyone."

> I think my desire to always get better, to always want more, to always be my top critic, and accepting the good and the bad."

> You have to fight to reach your dream. You have to sacrifice and work hard for it."

> I don't need the best hairstyle or the best body. Just give me a ball at

my feet, and I'll show you what I can do."

> " I want to be remembered as a good person rather than a good football player."

> " I always thought I wanted to play professionally, and I always knew that to do that, I'd have to make a lot of sacrifices."

> " I'm lucky to be part of a team who help to make me look good, and they deserve as much of the credit for my success as I do for the hard work we have all put in on the training ground."

BOOK
DISCUSSION

If you could meet Leo Messi, what is one question you would ask him, and why?

Leo is not just a football superstar; he gives back through his children's charity. What kind of charity would you like to start if you had the chance?

GET SMART ABOUT LIONEL MESSI

One of Leo's favorite hobbies is playing video games. How do you think this helped him with his football on the field?

_____
_____
_____
_____
_____

Leo knew from a very young age what he wanted to be when he grew up. What would you like to be when you grow up and why?

_____
_____
_____
_____
_____
_____
_____

GLOSSARY

advisor: /uhd-vahy-zer/ noun: someone who gives advice or helps you with information or guidance *<example: My teacher is a helpful advisor; she gives me advice on my school projects.>*

adapt: /uh-dapt/ verb: when you change and find new ways to do something to fit the situation *<example: Birds adapt to different weather by growing thicker feathers in the winter.>*

campaigned: /kam-peynd/ verb: when someone actively works to promote a cause or run for a position, like in an election *<example: He campaigned to win the student council election, talking to classmates and sharing his ideas.>*

charity: /cher-i-tee/ noun: when people or organizations help others in need, often by giving money, goods, or their time *<example: Donating to a charity helps provide food and clothing to those less fortunate in our community.>*

cuisine: /kwi-zeen/ noun: a style of cooking or food preparation, often associated with a specific region or culture *<example: Italian cuisine is famous for its pasta and pizza.>*

dedication: /ded-i-key-shuhn/ noun: when you work really hard and put a lot of effort into something *<example: Her dedication to practicing the piano every day made her a great musician.>*

determined: /dee-TUR-mind/ adjective: when you decide to do something and work really hard to make it happen <example: *She was determined to finish the puzzle, so she kept trying until all the pieces fit together.*>

disorder: /dis-OR-der/ noun: when things are not in the right order and can be messy or confused <example: *The messy room was a disorder, with toys everywhere.*>

disruption: /dis-ruhp-shuhn/ noun: when something interrupts or changes the normal way of doing things <example: *The loud noise caused a disruption in our class, making it hard to concentrate on our lessons.*>

division: /dih-vizh-uhn/ noun: when something is separated or split into parts <example: *The division of the*

cake into equal slices made it easy to share with everyone.>

excel: /ik-sel/ verb: when you are very good at something or do it better than others *<example: She worked hard to excel in her studies and got top grades in her class.>*

hesitated: /hez-i-tey-tid/ verb: when you stop or pause before doing something *<example: She hesitated before jumping into the cold water.>*

humility: /hyoo-mil-i-tee/ noun: when someone is modest and doesn't show off or act better than others *<example: His humility made him well-liked by everyone; he never bragged about his achievements.>*

icon: /ahy-kon/ noun: a symbol or person who is widely recognized and represents something special or important *<example: Mickey Mouse is an icon of Disney, known and loved by people all over the world.>*

impressive: /im-pres-iv/ adjective: when something makes a strong and positive impact, often because it's really good or big *<example: The fireworks display on the Fourth of July was truly impressive, with bright colors and loud pops in the night sky.>*

influence: /ˈin-flu-əns/ noun: when someone or something has the power to change the way you think or act *<example: Her excitement for reading influenced me to start reading too.>*

injections: /in-JEK-shuhns/ noun: when the doctor gives you medicine with a special needle to make you feel better

<example: The nurse gave me an injection to help me when I was sick.>

intense: /in-tens/ adjective: when something is very strong or extreme, often causing strong feelings or reactions *<example: The thunderstorm was so intense that it made everyone stay inside until it passed.>*

motivated: /moh-tuh-vey-tid/ adjective: when you feel excited and eager to do something *<example: He was motivated to finish his homework so he could go play outside.>*

mute: /myoot/ adjective: when something doesn't make a sound or is quiet *<example: The mute button on the remote makes the sound go away.>*

potential: /puh-ten-shuhl/ noun: when you have the ability to do something well in the future <example: With hard work and practice, you can reach your full potential and achieve your goals.>

prestigious: /pri-stij-uhs/ adjective: when something is respected and admired because it's considered important or of high quality *<example: Graduating from a prestigious university can open up many opportunities in your career.>*

propel: /prə-'pel/ verb: to make something move faster <example: The strong wind can propel a kite into the sky.>

setback: /set-bak/ noun: when something doesn't go as planned and you face a challenge or obstacle *<example: Missing the school bus was a*

setback, but I decided to walk to school instead.>

showcased: /shoh-kayst/ verb: when something is displayed or presented for others to see and enjoy *<example: The art gallery showcased beautiful paintings by local artists.>*

stable: /ˈstā-bəl/ adjective: when something doesn't change or wobble *<example: The table is stable; it doesn't shake when you touch it.>*

undeniable: /uhn-di-nahy-uh-buhl/ adjective: when something is impossible to deny or argue against *<example: The evidence presented in the case was undeniable; it clearly proved his guilt.>*

SELECTED REFERENCES

Balagué, G. (2013). Messi. Orion Books. ISBN 978-1-4091-4659-9.
Caioli, L. (2012). Messi: The Inside Story of the Boy Who Became a Legend. Corinthian Books. ISBN 978-1-906850-40-1.

Caioli, L. (2015). Messi: More than a Superstar. Icon Books. ISBN 978-1-906850-91-3.
Corrigan, D. (15 November 2013). "Messi Reflects on Debut 10 Years On." ESPN.

"FIFA" (5 March 2006). "The New Messiah." FIFA. Archived from the original on 21 October 2014.

Fitzpatrick, R. (23 June 2017). "The Machine of '87: Messi's Boyhood

Teammates Recall Early Signs of Greatness." Bleacher Report.

Guinness World Records 2015. (2014). Guinness World Records. ISBN 978-1-908843-65-4.

Henry, T. (21 April 2011). "The 2011 Time 100: Lionel Messi, God of the Field." Time.

Hunter, G. (2012). Barça: The Making of the Greatest Team in the World. BackPage Press. ISBN 978-0-9564971-8-5.

Laureus Sport Awards: Lionel Messi & Argentina World Cup team win Laureus awards. (8 May 2023). BBC Sport.

Lisi, C. A. (2011). A History of the World Cup: 1930–2010. Scarecrow Press. ISBN 978-0-8108-7754-2.

Longman, J. (21 May 2011). "Lionel Messi: Boy Genius." The New York Times.

"Profile: Lionel Andrés Messi." FC Barcelona. Retrieved 8 September 2015.

Williams, R. (24 February 2006). "Messi Has All the Qualities to Take World by Storm." The Guardian.

Maume, C. (11 July 2014). "Lionel Messi: The World at His Feet." The Independent. Archived from the original on 14 June 2022.

Messi. (n.d.). FC Barcelona.

Messi. (n.d.). Paris Saint-Germain F.C. 4 June 2023.

Messi Shares Baby Joy. (17 June 2012). beIN Sports. Archived from the original on 19 August 2015.

Lionel Messi: Player Profile. (n.d.). ESPN FC. Retrieved 9 September 2015.

Messi, L. (n.d.). FC Barcelona.

Messi, L. (n.d.). Paris Saint-Germain F.C. 4 June 2023.

LETTER FROM THE AUTHOR

Dear Readers,

I hope you enjoyed this book and learned some take away that may help you as you continue to grow and make choices in life. Legends and icons can teach us about what we want to do and what we might not want to do. They can help us learn about ourselves and what decisions help and hurt people as they follow their dreams. If you enjoyed learning about this icon, you could read about more in our kids biographies series!

Happy learning and may your dreams come true!

All the best,
Adam Kent

GET SMART ABOUT LIONEL MESSI

ADAM KENT

COLLECT THE WHOLE *GET SMART* BOOK SERIES

Here are just a few:

ROCKET BOOKS

Join our book club for free book offers. For more info email:

info@rocketkidsbookclub.com

Printed in Great Britain
by Amazon